THE GOLFER'S WAY

LESSONS IN A GAME

JUSTIN GILG

Copyright ©2025 by Justin Gilg

All rights reserved.

No portion of this book may be reproduced in any form without written permission from the publisher or author, except as permitted by U.S. copyright law.

Book Cover by Isabel Cano

First edition, 2025

Contents

Prologue	2
Walk the Earth	9
Take only what you can carry	11
Set an intention	13
Plan for variation	15
Welcome the elements	17
All separation is false	19
Experiment with variety	21
Play it where it lies	23
Embrace uncertainty	25
Timelessness	27
Visualize the next step	29
There is no destination	31
Practice mindfulness	33
Pause and breathe	35

Imagination	37
Practice 'non-doing'	39
Cultivate inspired action	41
Release all expectations	43
Less is more	45
There is always another opportunity	47
Champion your environment	49
Quiet the mind	51
Let go of your ego	53
Manifest what is there	55
Don't overthink it	57
Back to front	59
Swing your swing	61
Control is a mirage	63
Integrate with the past	65
Re-set	67
Mental medicine	69
It is what it is	71
Recognize illusions	73
Put in the reps	75

Circle back to the fundamentals	77
All the work counts	79
Pressure	81
Trust the process	83
Trial and error	85
See the sunrise	87
Create to create	89
Love	91
Belief	93
Epilogue	95

To EB and M Sol

Prologue

Pebble Beach. The name brings all serious golfers chills. It's one of the best public courses on US soil. Anyone can play it. It rests next to the Pacific Ocean with some of the holes seeming to levitate above it. To play it would be a spiritual experience. Little did I know just how much so. My grandpa introduced me to golf when I was fairly young. He lived in another state so I would only see him once or twice a year. But when I did after age twelve, we would play on the small nine-hole course. There was just something about it. I was hooked. I start taking lessons and played through high school, working at a local golf course through college. I was decent but never great. It seemed I had plateaued, but I did enjoy it. Until I didn't. They say don't mix work with pleasure, and every time I was working at the course, I wished I was playing instead. So eventually I stopped playing as often. After graduating I thought I was supposed to work at a 'real' job, so I played even less. My days were spent climbing the corporate ladder, and my weekends trying to escape that fact. I thought I was happy, but

I knew I was not fulfilled. It was a cycle that would repeat for years and years. Until it didn't.

Golf, like life, does not care what you have done or what you will do. It exists only in the present. Each day you wake up you could be different from the previous day. You can try to swing a certain way or plan life a certain way, only to get caught a bit offline and in the woods. The margin of error for mastery is tiny. And it can leave you at any time if you don't respect it. If you try to force it, or control it, it will backfire and leave you frustrated and blocked. If you let it flow naturally, it will come around. The only thing that matters is what is directly in front of you.

What was in front of me was a new beginning. I was done with my so-called career I had stumbled into. I was determined to see what was on the other side. And so I did. Soon after I resigned, I took a trip to San Francisco. I decided I would rent a car and drive to Monterey and play Pebble Beach. I called and they had one tee time available first thing Monday. I took it and didn't look back. I played with four gentlemen from Japan. Their ages ranged from forty to seventy-five. The oldest made an eighty foot putt on number three. Nobody spoke a common language. I carried my own bag in peaceful serenity. It was misty out and the waves were crashing on the rocks. It felt surreal. It was timeless. I was walking where legends played and I could sense their presence. After the round, I was floating.

This was it. I fell back in love with the game. I had the desire to be the best I could be. This time I would put in all the effort needed to be a scratch player. I made a vow to myself to re-engage with the game and discover the truths in it for me along the way.

This book is not a traditional instruction manual. While there are occasional tips embedded in it, it is more a meditation or guide into what makes this game transcendent and timeless. Golf allows me to play in the unknown. It allows me a peek into another world of imagination and exploration, and awaken to the life lessons that seem to be interwoven within the game. Hope you enjoy.

"The most important shot in golf is your next one"

> Ben Hogan

"The real way to enjoy playing golf is to take pleasure not in the score but in the execution of the strokes."

> Bobby Jones

"Practice is the only golf advice that is good for everybody"

> Arnold Palmer

THE LESSONS

WALK THE EARTH

The game is designed for walking. Up and down the hills I go, carrying the weight. My body is moving toward each shot. My heart rate is higher, my mental focus is sharper and clearer on what I want to accomplish. I don't start and stop. Instead I am idling and ready for the next moment. I'm connected to the pace of the game. I'm activated in a continuous journey.

TAKE ONLY WHAT YOU CAN CARRY

When I was beginning, I used a small set. I skipped every other iron and carried a couple of wedges. My bag was lighter as I started to get more used to it. I did not weigh myself down with the unnecessary. When I was a more accomplished player, I played a smaller set as a challenge. There I learned how to hit harder and softer versions of my regular shot. This allowed me to be creative, for each shot was different from the last. And it all added up.

SET AN INTENTION

I practice with the purpose of preparing myself for the course. I pick out specific drills that rehearse a move I need to work on. Or I pick out a target, choose a shot shape, and work on executing that. I want to test myself on the range, so when it comes time to perform on the course I am used to the challenge and have all of the confidence to pull it off. Then it is just a matter of reps and attention to the moment. I practice this intention again and again.

Plan for Variation

Take enough club. Sometimes I am planning my carry distance for the best possible number instead of the more realistic one. So I take an extra club and swing aggressively but smoothly. Even if I slightly mishit it, I have a better chance at reaching the center of the green. When I plan for variation, I allow more chances for success. Soon my strikes will get more and more refined. There will be no need to take more clubs; I will just hit it the distance I need.

WELCOME THE ELEMENTS

The natural surroundings are part of the game. As I play I will encounter heat, cold, wind, and rain, to name a few. I will climb up and down hills, around trees and through tall grass. It's all part of the game. The conditions are what they are, and I learn to adjust to them as I venture along. There are no shortcuts nor would I want there to be. It's all part of the fun.

ALL SEPARATION IS FALSE

The game has three parts. The first part focuses on preparation. The second part on action. The third is integration. What I soon realized is that all three of these sections overlap to become the whole. There is no separation. When I'm playing well, the past, present, and future begin to merge into one field of consciousness and awareness ... which will take me into a state of creation and reflect back to me a merging of my mind, body, and soul.

EXPERIMENT WITH VARIETY

I like to try swings with the old 'woods'. The persimmon driver. The one the game was built on for the first two hundred years. The one that feels pure when I hit it 'on the screws'. The one that will not stray too far left or right. The one that trains my rhythm and artistry. I play the forward tees and swing freely. I create my own 'par' that I can work toward. I build games within the game.

Play it where it lies

Play the ball where it lies. It's easy to prop the ball up to improve your lie, but that takes away the essence of the sport. I will have good lies and bad lies. It's not up to me. I don't improve it but integrate with it. I embrace the challenge of it. And see where my skill and talent can take me. I use it to build resourcefulness and flexibility.

EMBRACE UNCERTAINTY

I hit each shot the best I can and then go chase it down. When I arrive at my new surroundings, I take stock and come up with a plan and move forward with my next action. Each time I play the game I have a chance to become more and more efficient and effortless. There will be days where I think I am going backward and days when everything syncs up. All of it becomes part of the journey. I give gratitude for all the little steps and proceed with joy.

TIMELESSNESS

When I'm practicing or playing, there is a sense that nothing else is important except the moment. It's freeing and allows me to transcend into another dimension altogether – one of flow, ease, and attention to the craft. As I engage, the concept of time becomes blurred. Past, present, and future thoughts begin to blend into one long present instant as I experience the peaks and valleys. This all happens at a subconscious level, but I sense it through flashes of awareness and attention.

VISUALIZE THE NEXT STEP

I try to picture the next shot. I use my mind as a tool of awareness to visualize what I want to see happen before the swing occurs. I tap into the essence around me and allow what is going to unfold. I don't worry about not seeing it right away; I let it come to me a moment later. Then I trust what I see and move forward.

THERE IS NO DESTINATION

The path my ball takes to each hole will be different every time. I hit the ball then I walk a path to it. Then I hit it again and find another path to it. No paths are alike each time I play. There will always be unique variations. There is no set path. Each round will be slightly different ... and the same. The steps that are presented to me are mine to follow and learn from.

PRACTICE MINDFULNESS

Putting is a mind game. I'm going to miss some, and I'm going to make some. It is important to establish a routine that works for me and that I can perform over and over. From beginning to end I establish a sequence I can repeat. This takes the guesswork out of it. It is simply the pattern to get the ball into the cup. I trust the process.

PAUSE AND BREATHE

I pay attention to my breath as I play. I notice it as I walk, before I swing, and as I wait. I realize that I can always center myself by taking a deep breath and exhaling slowly a few times. When I do this, I direct the mind to think about the breath, instead of the result of the past or next shot. Once my mind is calm, my body will be able to perform the repeatable motion of the swing effortlessly.

Imagination

I think of each shot as a blank canvas in which I'm allowed to create. High, low, or in between, I choose how I want the ball to go. The more I am present with this fact, the more creative I will become. I am designed to imagine and manifest. Golf allows me to activate and feed my imagination with each shot.

PRACTICE 'NON-DOING'

The game lives in the present state. Situations arise. To play each situation well, I can't focus on the past or future, just the present. The more I practice this moment-by-moment awareness, the better I play. Each shot is an opportunity to commit to being fully present and aware. Right before I swing, I take a pause and focus on my breath and the ball. Then I start the motion and get out of the way and let the club swing 'itself'.

CULTIVATE INSPIRED ACTION

If I am set up comfortably and trust the shot, the execution will come automatically. I will not always pull it off, but I will be closer than I think. Instead of worrying how to do it perfectly, I concentrate on the small steps that trigger the motion. Then proceed.

Release All Expectations

Before hitting a shot, I let go of all the extra thoughts in my mind. There will be plenty as I make last-minute calculations and assessments. I release them and let myself just be in the moment the seconds before I engage. When I do this, I let all my training take over, and the swing happens in sync and naturally.

Less is More

I build my swing from the impact position out. All great players achieve similar body and club position at impact. I study it and model it. Then find out how I get my own body and club into that sequence. It does not matter how the rest of the backswing and follow-through looks; I just need to find a path that will get me into the impact position. From there I can build the swing around it. I start small and practice arriving at the same point each time without tension. When achieved, the ball jumps off the clubface, and the finish is balanced and natural.

THERE IS ALWAYS ANOTHER OPPORTUNITY

Every now and then I will make a good swing, but the result will not be what I want. When this happens, I move on from the moment and try again. It is only a small setback in the grand scheme of things, and it should not be overblown. I don't hold onto the past. I take a deep breath and go forth. The next positive result is waiting for me.

CHAMPION YOUR ENVIRONMENT

I take in my surroundings as I play. All the different plants and animals that cross my path. They are part of the game. I give gratitude that I can experience this moment with them. I breathe it in. The grass, the trees, the water, the sun. All of it moving and all of it part of the whole picture. A living, breathing ecosystem.

QUIET THE MIND

Before each shot I stand a couple of feet behind the ball and take three deep breaths. I allow my exhale to be longer than my inhale. This will quiet the mind and allow me to focus on the task at hand. By the end of the third breath, I walk up, take my stance, and swing away. By consciously controlling my breath, my mind relaxes and my body simply executes the next swing.

LET GO OF YOUR EGO

The game challenges my ego's narrative of the player I think I am versus the player I am. It brings to the surface comparisons to perceived past successes or failures, and future imaginings of what could or should happen. When this occurs, I anchor myself in the present. I realize that with each shot, I am learning something. Each attempt builds knowledge. I temporarily abandon my ego and welcome a blissful state of awareness and service to honing my craft. It's about syncing my body and mind in the joyful pursuit of a well-played shot.

MANIFEST WHAT IS THERE

My thoughts will create the action, which creates a reality that is reflected back to me. The game touches my innate creativity and ability to manifest or uncover what is already there. It shows me my true nature, which is abundance and transcendence in every moment. That's why I love the game. That's why it's worth pursuing. That's why it helps raise my consciousness.

Don't overthink it

Once I commit to a shot, I go with it. I don't overthink it. My initial thought is usually the correct one. If I don't fully believe in what I am doing before the shot, it will not end up where I want it. I let the club go at impact. I don't slow the motion down. Once I am committed to the shot I want to hit, I trust and complete the swing. If I don't commit, the ball will not either.

BACK TO FRONT

I learn to play the course from the back to the front. I start at the green and play the scenario to the tee box. I think about where I want to leave it and how to get into that position. Like a game of billiards, I play for the next shot in terms of strategy. I can make adjustments along the way, but the game plan will be in place.

SWING YOUR SWING

In playing this game I begin to develop unique skills that work for me. I keep checking in on fundamentals, but I don't try to copy another player's exact technique. I have one unique, repeatable motion in me, and that is mine to uncover. The goal is to get the ball in the hole in as few attempts as I can, not to have a 'perfect' swing. How I get there is my own journey. It will be a bunch of trial and error until it clicks. Then it will be like it was there all the time.

CONTROL IS A MIRAGE

One day I don't know where the ball is going; the very next day I am in complete control. It's the nature of the ups and downs of the game. It teaches me that while I think I can be in control, I'm not. Each moment has its destiny. And if I string enough moments together, something great can happen. I allow and accept it as it's happening. I play within myself and watch what bubbles up.

INTEGRATE WITH THE PAST

I accept the shot result however it turns out. I cannot change it after it occurs; all I can do is learn from it and move on. The only part I can control is my reaction to it. I accept it and move on to the next one. I learn to recover from temporary setbacks and thrive on positive results.

Re-set

The game can serve as a great re-set. It can transform stuck energy into a higher frequency. As I play, I can detach from whatever circumstances are going on in my day to day and just be in the moment. To me the score is secondary; the real benefit is in the practice. The practice of exploration. The practice of creation. The practice of detaching from the outcome.

Mental Medicine

Each time I play I walk a new path that is familiar but completely different. An analog experience in a digital world. Engaging my senses in a direct physical encounter between me and what I'm experiencing. Tactile and challenging with joy as its by-product. To excel, I relax, trust, and release expectations. Then watch as my manifestations emerge.

IT IS WHAT IT IS

The score. It is used to track my baseline day to day or round by round, but it does not always equate to how I am playing. Some scores seem better than others, and vice versa. I don't get too attached to any one score or any one day. I let it be a guide instead of a detriment. The best days are when I forget about the score and just play each shot one by one. Then add it up afterward.

RECOGNIZE ILLUSIONS

The more I let go of trying to get better at the game, the better I become. This is not to be confused with practice and working on the craft. It is just in expectations. I will have moments when things click. Because I did it once, I expect it will happen again. I begin to reach for it. But that is all an illusion. There is no reaching for it again, because my next swing is new. So instead I let go of any expectations. Let go of any judgment and just play the game. If I keep at it, my baseline will move up. There is no *trying* to get there. There is just *doing* with no attachment.

PUT IN THE REPS

Big leaps will be made in this game if I keep playing. I will reach plateaus and then jump from one to the next. And back again. The good shots will always keep me coming back. This is the beauty of the game. Each shot is a potential for greatness. I keep making swings. Soon I will just be one with the moment and not thinking about anything. This is where the game can move me into another dimension altogether. One of presence.

CIRCLE BACK TO THE FUNDAMENTALS

Sometimes too many thoughts have entered my consciousness, and the game seems like I am beginning again. I hit shots thin and fat, I don't know which direction they are going. When this happens, I check the fundamentals. It may seem like I'm regressing, but it is just the adaption of a new movement that has not been completed yet. I am never as bad or good as I think. And progress is not in a straight line. The leaps forward are coming if I am patient. I go back to the beginning and keep faith in the process.

ALL THE WORK COUNTS

Everything I do adds up and compounds. I don't lose it. All the shots I previously hit help with the next one. All the practice and all the lessons are built into my subconscious. So each chance I have to play or practice, I am building something: knowledge, muscle memory, solutions in my personal database. The longer I work at it, the more I will uncover. The game is here to teach me mindfulness, awareness, and patience, if I let it.

Pressure

I play a match for stakes to see what pressure feels like. What posting a score feels like. What sifting through nervous energy feels like. What success feels like and what failure feels like. Everything counts and anything can happen. I will experience how my swing holds up to pressure. I will begin to understand which components did work and which did not. There are so many variables in my game, so it's good to realize which ones need more focus. Under pressure I find out what I'm confident in and what needs fine-tuning. Then I can let go and play.

TRUST THE PROCESS

There are no shortcuts. I move two steps forward then one step back. As I continue to tweak and fix one thing, another pops up. I don't concern myself with this. It is natural. It's what makes the game what it is. The key is to keep at it. Celebrate the successes and recognize and learn from the failures. I learn the lessons as I go and realize it's all part of the journey.

TRIAL AND ERROR

Occasionally I need to try different methods until I find the one that makes the most sense to me. Golf is a game of inches, and small adjustments can have a great impact. I can use this to my advantage as I build my skills. I'm not afraid to try something new to gain a different feel or understanding of how I can best play the game. Because there is so much variety in golf, the possibilities for experimentation are endless. For there is no final destination in my golf journey—it's a continuous path which I alone can author. Every day presents an opportunity to add to my repertoire. There are no failures, only increasing awareness of what truly works for me.

SEE THE SUNRISE

I wake up early. I walk and see the sun break through the clouds. I catch up with old friends. I hit some great shots. I make some putts. I take deep breaths, visualize, and manifest. I use my imagination as the game unfolds in front of me. Over and over again until I am finished. Once completed, I feel at ease. My work is done for the day. This is why I put in the practice. This is why I invest in myself and my game. The game pays me back in subtle ways I don't even comprehend. But I feel it. I feel alive and I feel at peace.

CREATE TO CREATE

The more I am motivated from within to improve, the easier the game becomes. I begin to practice and play because I want to, not because any outside force is prompting me to do so. I am just playing for the art, soul, and joy of it. When I allow myself to get into this headspace, I can thrive. For I am fostering intrinsic inspiration. As I see improvement, it becomes a closed-loop system that builds and builds.

Love

I forgive myself for perceived 'failed' shots. It is all a learning process. I keep remembering it is all about love. Love of the game, love for myself, and love for others. The game has room for all. I honor myself as I learn it. I embrace what comes up, and what it is teaching me. I observe my cadence and am grateful for the experiences.

Belief

I believe in myself. I know the next swing is going to be the swing I want. It all led up to this, so I let the past go. I believe the next shot is going to be great. Then I release all expectations of the moment and let my training take over. I allow the joy of creation to lead and, like magic, watch the ball disappear into the cup.

Epilogue

Not that long ago I went to my local course to establish a handicap. Since I was there, I thought I would play nine holes. I was paired with one other guy. He told me a story of trying to establish a handicap for his trip to St. Andrews. Part of the reason I wanted an approved handicap is because I wanted to visit Scotland and play the 'Old Course', the home of golf. It was a sign. I proceeded to play great. Later, when I started entering in the scores, it dawned on me that I have a much lower handicap than I thought. When I started this new golf journey years ago after playing Pebble Beach, I told myself I want to get below a two. After pugging in the numbers, it said I was there. I had done it.

A year or so later I was on the Old Course. I had won the singles lottery to walk on and join a group. A couple members welcomed me. I hit my first shot and we were off. A four-hour pilgrimage walking the natural, uneven, wild terrain. Out to sea and back home. The entire time feeling immense gratitude for where I had been, where I was, and where I was going.

ABOUT THE AUTHOR

Justin is a golf guide (Class A PGTAA Teaching Professional) and loves to share his learning's and experiences with others to help them play better golf. *The Golfer's Way: Lessons in a Game* is his third book. You can read more of his writings and reach him at jmgbooks.com.

ALSO BY JUSTIN GILG (JMG)

Grounding from Within: Musings on Truth, Discipline, Attachment and Joy

Moving Beyond: Musings on Solitude, Awareness, and Manifestation

Made in the USA
Coppell, TX
17 January 2026